M000081804

THE
DA VINCI
DOG

THE
DA VINCI
DOG

The passion, paintings & slobber of Brinks the Dog

Paul Amelchenko

WILLOW CREEK PRESS

Published by Willow Creek Press
P.O. Box 147, Minocqua, Wisconsin 54548

For information on other Willow Creek Press titles,
call 1-800-850-9453

Editor: Andrea Donner
Design: Donnie Rubo

Printed in Canada

FOR JINGLES

PORTRAIT OF THE ARTIST

....

Since July 2005, Brinks Amelchenko has been painting everyday—mostly in the mornings, sometimes in the evenings, and always on the windows of his owners' French doors. These doors are his canvas, his nose the brush, and the world around him his inspiration.

....

"Before July 2005, I had never even thought about painting or sculpting. Then I was dropped off at the Humane Society of Broward County. The three days I spent there really changed me. I mean that literally, because they neutered me and tattooed my crotch. But I also mean that mentally. The experience gave me a new perspective on who I was as a dog, and more importantly, who I was as an artist."

Despite the technical mastery of his work, Brinks has no formal training— aside from a stint with Bark Busters Obedience School where he learned to sit, stay, and stop jumping up on people.

Crazy Ex-Squirrel-Friend, slobber on glass, 9x12"
Much of the artist's work is about confronting the issues.
Especially when the issues are squirrels.

Brinks' natural talent has caused some to deem him a prodigy of the art world —a sort of four-legged wunderkind. Despite the attention, the artist insists that he remains well grounded.

"I don't get carried away with attention to my work," says Brinks. "Attention to me on the other hand, well that's another story. Especially when it involves cookies and belly rubs."

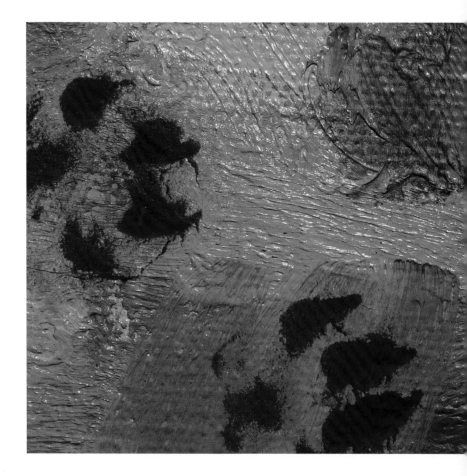

French Door Paintings

....

Few artists are as committed as Brinks Amelchenko. Religiously, he communes with the canvas each morning, fueled by pure passion, artistic vision, and 2½ cups of Science Diet Venison and Potatoes.

....

....

"Squirrels—*Someday I'll Get You* really began as a series of individual works detailing my uncontrollable excitement, my desire to retrieve, and my ability to slobber up a clean window in a matter of seconds," says Brinks.

The following works were completed from November 2005 through July 2006.

....

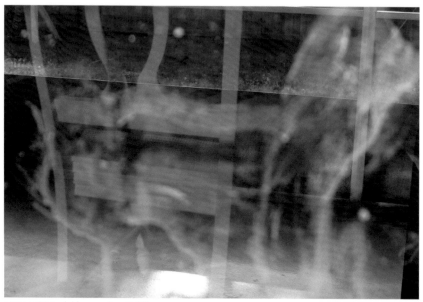

Let me at 'em, slobber on glass, 9x12"

"*Let me at 'em* was one of my early experimental studies. I had recently returned from a morning walk and settled by the window with my rawhide. I spotted a squirrel running along the fence, and I just went berserk—barking and drooling and spinning frantically."

"When the squirrel disappeared and I settled down, I realized what I had created. It was brilliant—a true masterpiece. From that moment I was inspired and driven, and I spent the rest of the morning—and the rest of every morning actually—barking and slobbering... and creating."

Furry breakfast, slobber on glass, 9x12″

....

"*Furry breakfast* is one of my more thoughtful pieces. For me, it's really just as much a commentary on post modern theory as it is a declaration of my love for double-basted rawhide twisties. Both concepts are recurring themes in much of my work, but I think that's fairly obvious—even to the casual art fan."

....

A new day, Time to play, slobber on glass, 9x12"

....

"*A new day, Time to play* is one of my personal favorites. The evening before I created this piece, our cleaning lady had meticulously Windex-ed each pane in the door. I hadn't realized at the time because I was running around with her rubber gloves in my mouth. But when I awoke the next morning and approached my canvas, I was greeted with a blank slate— a *'tabula rasa'* if you will."

....

A new day, Time to play (left) and *The same day, Still time to play* (right)
Designed as complementary pieces, they remain equally striking as individual works.

....

"To some artists, the empty canvas is intimidating. To me, it's invigorating. This is my follow up to *A new day, Time to play* entitled *The same day, Still time to play.*"

....

*The same day, **Still time to play***, slobber on glass, 9x12"

....

"*The same day, Still time to play* was about getting my individual voice to arise. Unfortunately, at one point, it arose too loudly and Paul and Stacey, my owners, made me lie down and be quiet for a while. But as any artist will tell you, passion is persistent, and it was only a matter of minutes before I was overcome with artistic exuberance— and the need to poop. So Paul let me run around in the backyard before returning to my easel."

....

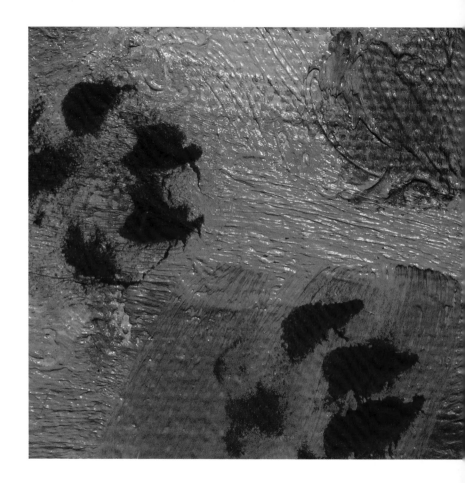

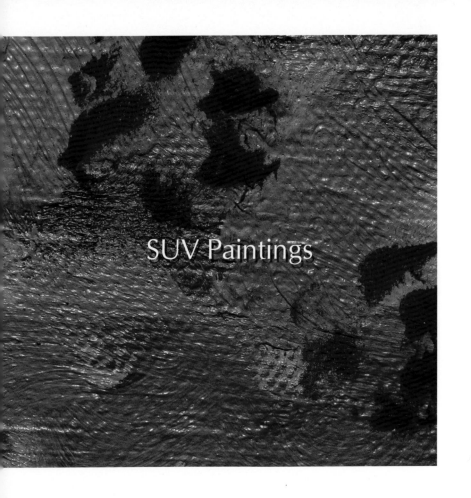

SUV Paintings

....

"**Although I do most of my painting in the studio, I also find great inspiration outdoors—**particularly in Paul's Explorer. The excitement of seeing new neighborhoods, and the open highway really gets my creative juices flowing—especially those clear juices that dribble from my nose and mouth."

....

....

"While the car is in motion, I often find it difficult to achieve the technical detail that I'm known for. So as we drive, I use that time to think and visualize and lick Paul's ears. That way, when we reach a stop sign or a red light, I'm focused and ready to produce."

"Just like in my home studio, I usually work on three to four canvases at a time —sketching a little on each one, walking in circles, wagging my tail, and then returning to each canvas as I see fit—or as I see birds—whichever happens first."

....

West Palm Beach series

"The following pieces were created in June of 2006 as I was traveling to West Palm Beach. Paul and Stacey were vacationing and dropping me off at Very Important Paws, a fashionable dog hotel. I was very excited at the time, drooling, panting—I think my lipstick may have even been out. In any case, I think that excitement and enthusiasm is evident in my brushstrokes."

"This is an abstract of my friend Foster, titled simply *Foster*. We play non-stop until I start humping him and get placed in time-out."

Foster, slobber on UV-coated glass, 3x1'
This abstract depicts a return to 'puppyhood'
that is often followed by a return to 'time out'.

"**These two pieces are action portraits of my friend Champ and I. In the piece,** *Masterminds***,** we're discussing our upcoming plans for the week. In the painting, *Play Day*, we're chasing each other in circles."

Masterminds, slobber on UV-coated glass, 3x1'
These action portraits illustrate the inner
workings of the artist's mind.

Play Day, slobber on UV-coated glass, 3x1'

"You can see in both *The Car, The Car, The Car* and *Can I go? Can I go? Can I go?* how my brushstrokes are significantly rougher and less refined than my other works—even my early experimental pieces. I debated whether or not to include these in my portfolio, but they represent a turning point in my career as an artist, and really became the catalyst that opened me up to new techniques outside of painting."

The Car, The Car, The Car
slobber on UV-coated glass, 3x1'

Can I go? Can I go? Can I go?
slobber on UV-coated glass, 3x1'

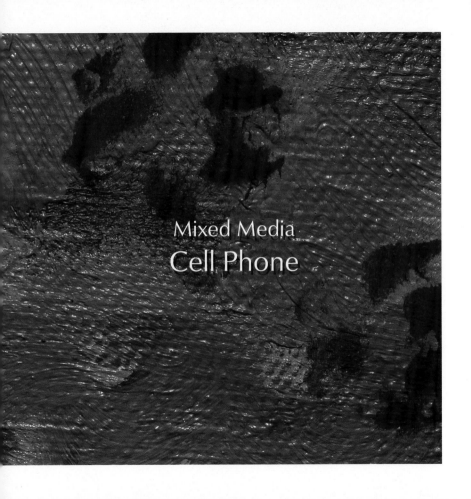

Mixed Media
Cell Phone

....

"**Although I'm a painter at heart, on occasion, I'll experiment with different media.** I find art everywhere—in the sunrise, in the grass, and in this case, on the coffee table."

....

"Paul and I were watching TV in the living room one morning. During a commercial break, he went into the kitchen for a glass of water and left his cell phone on the table. As I watched him leave the room, I glanced down to see his blue T-Mobile just begging to be shaped and molded."

Cell Phone Surprise, Samsung SGH-R225M, 4.25x2.25"
This sculpture brilliantly depicts the artist's need to communicate.

....

"This particular piece was actually completed in a matter of seconds. I immediately punctured the liquid crystal screen with my front tooth, creating a colorful starburst effect. The way the bluish-hues and rainbow colors contrast with the spider-webbed plastic really pulls the work together."

....

....

"I'll be the first to admit that I tend to overwork a piece sometimes, especially when working with plastics. Fortunately for me, Paul returned with his water in less than a minute, and told me I was finished sculpting for the morning."

....

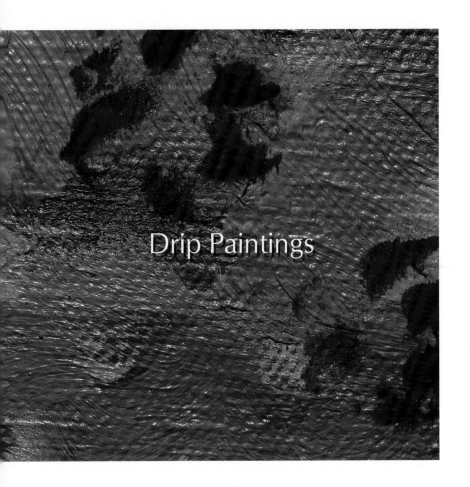

Drip Paintings

Like many artists, Brinks often finds his muse while focused on other activities —strolling the avenue, gazing at stars, or licking dirty silverware in the dishwasher. Recently he found inspiration while enjoying a drink at his "dog bar"—a fitting location perhaps, considering the "intoxicating" nature of his work.

"**I try to keep most of my artwork from becoming too political, but water conservation is an issue I feel very passionately about.** I believe there is far too much of this "conservation" taking place, and if it were up to me, water would be everywhere."

The artist's vision of 'aquatic abundance' is the driving force behind his latest series of drip paintings.

....

"Jackson Pollock was one of the world's most prominent drip painters and I make no attempt to disguise his influence in my art."

"The main difference between our work isn't so much in style, but in medium. While Pollock worked mainly on canvas, I prefer to work on tile—especially Stacey's kitchen tile."

....

Half Full, Half Empty, Half on the Floor, filtered spring water on ceramic tile, 3x3'
By including three 'halves' in his title, the artist reminds us that conventions must
be challenged and that dogs can't count very well.

Paul Almost Fell, filtered spring water on ceramic tile, 4x6'

"**I find that a canvas can be confining**, while tile allows me to literally —and figuratively—spread my composition and my convictions beyond the kitchen and into the dining room, the living room, and occasionally even the hallway."

Conservation Termination, filtered spring water and melted ice cube on ceramic tile, 4x6'

"**Mobilizing the masses isn't easy.** Sometimes I'll look at a piece like *Conservation Termination* and wonder 'Is this the best I can do? Will it inspire others? How long 'til dinner?' It can be difficult to focus, but I know that the more people I can touch with my ideas the sooner we can bring an end to water conservation."

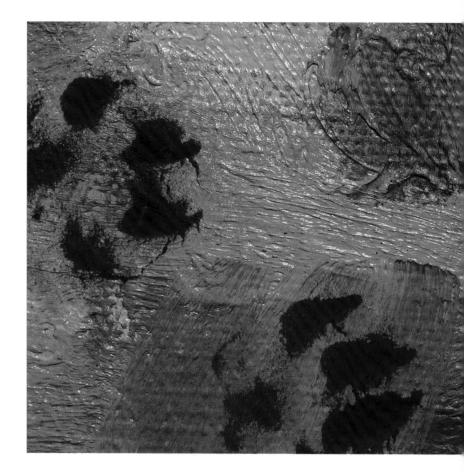

Mixed Media
Poop Bags

....

"**As an artist, few things get me more excited than an empty poop bag**, mainly because it means I'm going for a walk somewhere."

"For me, poop bags are a symbol of liberation, and momentum—not to mention the chance to see Peaches, the pretty yellow Lab who lives around the corner. Ironically, these figures of freedom are stored in dark, cramped quarters under the bench in our hallway."

....

"**On a Saturday last spring, I noticed that one of these poop bags was peering out from under the bench**. I could hear it crying out for freedom, I imagine in much the same way that David cried out to Michelangelo. Stacey was too busy in the kitchen to hear it, so I pulled it free."

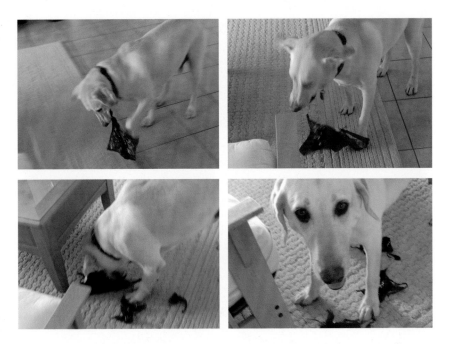

"The entire experience was very liberating, and caused me to reflect...
had I discovered a new medium? Should I shift my focus to performance
art? And why didn't Michelangelo use more poop bags?"

Mixed Media
Toilet Paper Roll

"**After my morning walk, while Paul is in the shower, I sit next to the tub and contemplate my day**. One morning I was feeling especially grateful for the time that we had shared, so I decided to sculpt him a present."

"This piece was finished rather quickly so it lacks some of the detail I had hoped to achieve. It's called *I haven't eaten breakfast yet* and it was, more or less, a reminder to Paul that, well, I hadn't eaten breakfast yet... and that I was hungry."

I haven't eaten breakfast yet, 300 sheet 2-ply roll, 4.5x4"

....

"At first, Paul didn't comprehend the piece. That's because he doesn't usually feed me; Stacey does, but she went to work early that day. So it was Paul's job and he wasn't moving fast enough. So while Paul was getting dressed, I continued working with additional design elements that had fallen to the floor."

....

....

"To me, the tattered, two-ply roll is an obvious metaphor for my stomach's spiraling journey into hunger. On the left, one can see a robust full belly that is happy and satisfied. And on the right, a thinning, famished canine that hasn't eaten for several hours... except of course for a few cookies and a liver snap or two."

....

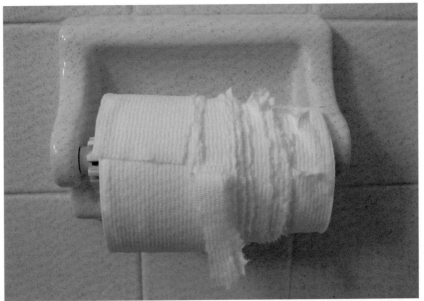

I haven't eaten breakfast yet demonstrates the artist's cry for nourishment

"With the quilted remnants of my sculpture, I created a supporting piece. The style is a distinctive mix of abstract expressionism and primitive origami. The figural representations depict Paul feeding me, and me jumping into the air. Then they show me walking back to the bathroom, climbing into the tub, and rolling around on the wet tile."

Carousel of Hunger, toilet paper on tile, 8x8"

Mixed Media
Palm Frond Sculpture

....

The Palm Frond Sculpture

"This piece was actually my first attempt at woodworking."

"I was helping Paul in the backyard. He had just finished cutting the grass, weeding the yard, and trimming several palm trees. I was on the porch cleaning out the drip cup under the barbecue when I noticed him carrying an armful of palm fronds. Even though I was busy, I knew he needed help so I ran up behind him and yanked the pile to the ground."

....

Memoirs of the Palm, areca palm frond, 6′

....

"As Paul chased me, shouting words of encouragement like "stay" and "stop," I began ripping each leaf off the branch—one at a time. Before long, I had covered most of the newly cleaned yard with shredded palm leaves."

....

Memoirs of the Palm represents the artist's return to primal
storytelling, followed by his return to the barbecue.

"For me, the experience was about more than simply helping Paul. It was about listening to nature, and helping the leaves to tell their story. Then it was about ripping those leaves in half, eating them, and running back to the barbecue to finish licking the drip cup."

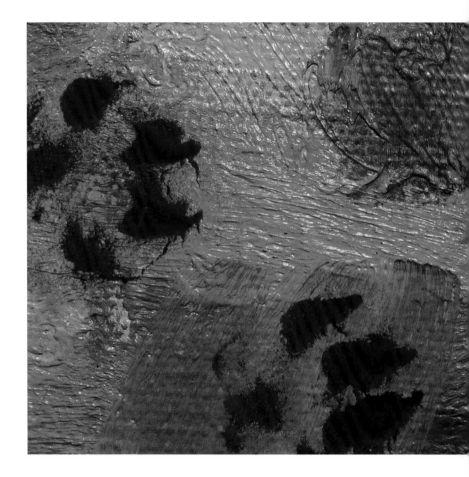

Totem Fence

"**The success of *Memoirs of the Palm* catapulted me into an exciting period of woodworking**. My fascination with the medium was elevated one afternoon while chewing a book on totem poles. Even though I had only chewed the first two-thirds of chapter one and most of the spine before being discovered, it was enough to propel me forward artistically."

TOTEM POLE

HOYT-GOLDSMITH

LAWRENCE MIGDALE

....

"While eating the book, I learned that certain Native Americans carved poles with family crests or mythical characters, and displayed them in front of their homes. I also learned that the book was a present for one of Stacey's friends, that it cost $20, and that I would not be enjoying a rawhide that evening. Nevertheless, I was excited about my newfound knowledge."

....

"**When I awoke the next morning, I was determined to embark on a bold creative endeavor.** And that's exactly what I did when the neighbor's dog, Hershey, appeared on the other side of the fence."

"**Hershey was snarling and barking ferociously**. But instead of joining in this behavior, as I typically do, I harnessed my emotions, redirected my energies, and began carving a totem fence."

Totem Fence, board-on-board lumber carvings, 8x6'
The intricately whittled etchings in *Totem Fence*
virtually bring the work to life.

....

"At first glance, this piece can seem overwhelmingly provocative, and in many ways it is. But it's also intended to soothe the senses, to pacify the mind, and to let Hershey know that I'm the boss of the neighborhood."

"All these designs were done by hand, except the deeper chips and large splinters, which were done by tooth."

....

Totem Fence pays homage to the circadian
rhythms of nature and the neighbor's dog.

....

"**Like much of my work, Totem Fence is an ongoing project**. It continually evolves according to my moods, my energy level, and whether or not Hershey is outside."

....

....

"**For me, it's the dynamic nature of the piece that makes it so special**. In many ways, *Totem Fence* is a visual diary of my evolution as an artist, depicting not only where I've been, but more importantly, where I'm going. Which, of course, I always hope is in the car."

....

What lies ahead for Brinks Amelchenko? "Well, I'm excited about a lot of things. Lately I've been experimenting with dirt. Mud in particular. Digging in it, rolling in it, eating it. And of course, living in Florida, I'm fascinated with lizards. Could they be my next big source of inspiration? It's possible. But right now, I've still got plenty of squirrels running around in my head."